How to Analyze the Roles of

PAUL
NEWMAN

by Sue Vander Hook

ABDO
Publishing Company

Essential Critiques

How to Analyze the Roles of

PAUL
NEWMAN

by Sue Vander Hook

Content Consultant: Dr. Maureen Turim
Professor of English and Film and Media Studies, University of Florida

Credits

Published by ABDO Publishing Company, 8000 West 78th Street, Edina, Minnesota 55439. Copyright © 2011 by Abdo Consulting Group, Inc. International copyrights reserved in all countries. No part of this book may be reproduced in any form without written permission from the publisher. The Essential Library™ is a trademark and logo of ABDO Publishing Company.

Printed in the United States of America,
North Mankato, Minnesota
062010
092010

 THIS BOOK CONTAINS AT LEAST 10% RECYCLED MATERIALS.

Special thanks to Susan Hamen, contributing author for chapters 4 and 8.
Editor: Amy Van Zee
Copy Editor: David Johnstone
Interior Design and Production: Marie Tupy
Cover Design: Marie Tupy

Library of Congress Cataloging-in-Publication Data
Vander Hook, Sue, 1949-
  How to analyze the roles of Paul Newman / Sue Vander Hook.
     p. cm. — (Essential critiques)
  Includes bibliographical references.
  ISBN 978-1-61613-532-4
1. Newman, Paul, 1925-2008—Criticism and interpretation—Juvenile literature.
2. Film criticism—Juvenile literature. I. Title.
  PN2287.N44V36 2010
  791.4302'8092—dc22
                                        2010015755

Table of Contents

1

Introduction to Critiques

What Is Critical Theory?

What do you usually do as a member of an audience during a movie? You probably enjoy the setting, the costumes, and the sound track. You learn about the characters as they are developed through dialogue and other interactions. You might be drawn in by the plot of the movie, eager to find out what happens next. Yet these are only a few of many possible ways of understanding and appreciating a movie. What if you are interested in delving more deeply? You might want to learn more about an actor and how his or her personal background is reflected in the film. Or you might want to examine what the film says about society—how it depicts the roles of women and minorities, for example. If so, you have entered the realm of critical theory.

Critical theory helps you learn how various works of art, literature, music, theater, film, and other endeavors either support or challenge the way society behaves. Critical theory is the evaluation and interpretation of a work using different philosophies, or schools of thought. Critical theory can be used to understand all types of cultural productions.

There are many different critical theories. If you are analyzing a movie, each theory asks you to look at the work from a different perspective. Some theories address social issues, while others focus on the actor's life or the time period in which the movie was written or set. For example, the critical theory that asks how an actor's life affected the work is called biographical criticism. Other common schools of criticism include historical criticism, feminist criticism, psychological criticism, and New Criticism, which examines a work solely within the context of the work itself.

What Is the Purpose of Critical Theory?

Critical theory can open your mind to new ways of thinking. It can help you evaluate a film from a new perspective, directing your attention to issues and messages you may not otherwise recognize in a work. For example, applying feminist criticism to a film may make you aware of female stereotypes perpetuated in the work. Applying a critical theory to a work helps you learn about the person who created it or the society that enjoyed it. You can explore how the film is perceived by current cultures.

How Do You Apply Critical Theory?

You conduct a critique when you use a critical theory to examine and question a work. The theory you choose is a lens through which you can view the work, or a springboard for asking questions about the work. Applying a critical theory helps you to think critically about the work. You are free to question the work and make an assertion about it. If you choose to examine a movie using biographical theory, for example, you want to know how the director's personal background or education inspired or shaped the work. You could explore why the director was drawn to the story. For instance, are there any parallels between a particular character's life and the director's life?

Forming a Thesis

Ask your question and find answers in the work or other related materials. Then you can create a thesis. The thesis is the key point in your critique. It is your argument about the work based on the tenets, or beliefs, of the theory you are using. For example, if you are using biographical theory to ask how the director's life inspired the work, your thesis could be worded as follows: Teng Xiong, raised in refugee camps in southeast Asia, drew upon her experiences to write, direct, and act in the film *No Home for Me*.

> **How to Make a Thesis Statement**
>
> In a critique, a thesis statement typically appears at the end of the introductory paragraph. It is usually only one sentence long and states the author's main idea.

Providing Evidence

Once you have formed a thesis, you must provide evidence to support it. Evidence might take the form of examples and quotations from the work itself—such as dialogue from a movie. Articles about the film or personal interviews with the director or actors might also support your ideas. You may wish to address what other critics have written about the work. Quotes from these individuals may help support your claim. If you find any quotes or examples that contradict your thesis, you will need to create an argument against them. For instance: Many critics have pointed to the heroine of *No Home for Me* as a powerless victim of circumstances. However, she is clearly depicted as someone who seeks to shape her own future.

How to Support a Thesis Statement

A critique should include several arguments. Arguments support a thesis claim. An argument is one or two sentences long and is supported by evidence from the work being discussed.

Organize the arguments into paragraphs. These paragraphs make up the body of the critique.

In This Book

In this book, you will read overviews of famous films Paul Newman starred in, each followed by a critique. Each critique will use one theory and apply it to one work. Critical thinking sections will give you a chance to consider other theses and questions about the work. Did you agree with the author's application of the theory? What other questions are raised by the thesis and its arguments? You can also find out what other critics think about each particular film. Then, in the You Critique It section in the final pages of this book, you will have an opportunity to create your own critique.

Look for the Guides

Throughout the chapters that analyze the works, thesis statements have been highlighted. The box next to the thesis helps explain what questions are being raised about the work. Supporting arguments have been underlined. The boxes next to the arguments help explain how these points support the thesis. Look for these guides throughout each critique.

Paul Newman began acting when he was a child.

2

A Closer Look at Paul Newman

People remember Paul Newman for his captivating charm, his wit, his stubbornness, and his nonconformity. In his career, Newman acted in theater productions, television shows, and films, as well as directed and produced movies. At age 61, he won an Academy Award for Best Actor for his 1986 performance as Fast Eddie Felson in *The Color of Money*. He received eight other Academy Award nominations, three Golden Globe Awards, and numerous other honors.

Boy from Ohio

Paul Newman was born on January 26, 1925, in upscale Shaker Heights, Ohio. His mother, Theresa Fetzer Newman, was Slovakian. His father, Arthur

Samuel Newman, was Jewish, the son of Polish and
Hungarian immigrants.

Paul began acting at age seven. He played
the court jester in his school's production of *The
Travails of Robin Hood*. When Paul was 11, his
mother enrolled him in Curtain Pullers, an acting
program for children at the famous Cleveland Play
House. In high school, Paul became interested in the
school drama program.

College, War, and Broadway

After high school, Newman took classes at
Ohio University and then served in the navy during
World War II. After the war, Newman attended
Kenyon College in Ohio, graduating in 1949. That
year, he married Jackie Witte. Paul and Jackie had
three children. In 1954, Newman graduated from
Yale University with a degree in drama. He also
studied at the Actors Studio in New York City.
Newman's professional acting career began on
Broadway with the stage production of *Picnic*.
Audiences liked the play, which ran for 14 months,
had 477 performances, and won a Pulitzer Prize.
Newman appeared in two other Broadway shows:
The Desperate Hours and *Sweet Bird of Youth*.

Motion Pictures

By the end of 1954, 29-year-old Newman was in Hollywood, California, acting in his first movie, *The Silver Chalice*. Movie critics were brutal and gave it poor reviews. Newman thought he played a terrible leading role as Basil and later apologized publicly in a newspaper advertisement for his poor performance.

Two years later, in 1956, Newman played professional boxer Rocky Graziano in *Somebody Up There Likes Me*. To learn about fighting, he spent his days at a gymnasium and trained alongside Graziano himself. Newman learned how to box, but most of all he studied how Graziano talked and how he moved. It was typical of Newman: He studied, he learned, and he imitated to become the best at the role he was playing.

Newman was experiencing personal problems at the time. His seven-year marriage to Jackie was strained, and his attraction to actress Joanne Woodward had the potential for scandal. Newman's marriage ended in divorce, and in 1958, he and Joanne married. That marriage would last 50 years, and the two would have three daughters. The couple appeared together in numerous films.

Rise to Fame

In 1958, Newman starred with Elizabeth Taylor in the popular movie *Cat on a Hot Tin Roof*. It received mixed reviews and a fair amount of criticism because it did not follow the entire plot of the original Tennessee Williams play on which it was based.

Some of Newman's movies of the 1960s included *The Hustler* (1961), *Hud* (1963), *Hombre* (1967), *Cool Hand Luke* (1967), and *Butch Cassidy and the Sundance Kid* (1969). The 1960s were a tough time for movies, as television was increasingly keeping more people at home and away from movie theaters. But Newman's performances as a shameful son in *Hud*, an outcast in *Hombre*, and a savvy rebel in *Cool Hand Luke* brought him even more fame and sealed his status as a celebrity.

Not all of Newman's movies in the 1960s were popular. Critics claimed that Newman was miscast in many of his roles. But when he was cast in the right role, Newman's popularity soared. In both 1964 and 1966, Newman won the Golden Globe Henrietta Award for World Film Favorite—Male.

In 1967, Newman starred as a convict and a nonconforming loner in what many consider

Paul Newman and his wife Joanne Woodward attended the premiere of *Cool Hand Luke* in 1967.

his best film: *Cool Hand Luke*. By the end of the decade, his popularity had grown even more. His 1969 performance as a charming, witty Old West bandit in *Butch Cassidy and the Sundance Kid* made him a superstar. The film was a blockbuster.

Race Car Driver

In 1969, Newman and Woodward teamed up to star in *Winning*, a film about professional race car driver Frank Capua, whom Newman played in the film. Newman drove his own race car for portions of the movie, which was filmed at the Indianapolis Motor Speedway. To prepare for his part, Newman trained with race car drivers. Newman's personal interest in the world of racing was sparked by his role in the movie. Three years after the film, in 1972, 44-year-old Newman began racing professionally in real life. Five years after that, he raced in the 24-hour Le Mans, taking second place in his Porsche 935.

Until the early 1990s, Newman drove for the Bob Sharp Racing Team. He eventually walked away with several racing championships and owned his own racing team as well as a NASCAR Winston Cup car. It was a lifelong interest for the actor.

Newman's films of the early 1970s secured his place as a Hollywood star. In 1982, Newman starred as Frank Galvin in *The Verdict*. For his performance, he received an Academy Award nomination for Best Actor and a Golden Globe Award nomination for Best Actor in a Motion Picture Drama. But it was his 1986 role as Fast Eddie Felson in *The Color of Money* that won the 62-year-old Newman his first Academy Award for Best Actor. He also received a Golden Globe Award nomination for Best Actor.

Later Works

Newman acted in five films in the 1990s, including *Nobody's Fool* (1994), for which he was nominated for an Academy Award and a Golden Globe Award for Best Actor. In 2002, he played opposite Tom Hanks in a role as a mob boss in the film *Road to Perdition*. For that performance, he received nominations for Best Supporting Actor for the Academy Awards, the British Academy of Film and Television Arts Awards, and the Golden Globe Awards. At the age of 78, Newman appeared in a Broadway theater production of Thornton Wilder's *Our Town*, for which he received a Tony Award nomination.

In 2006, Newman was the voice of retired race car Doc Hudson in the popular Disney animated film *Cars*. The following year, Newman narrated the documentary film *Dale*, the story of the life and career of professional race car driver Dale Earnhardt.

Philanthropist

Newman's personal life was just as successful as his acting career. He was a philanthropist, giving more than $250 million to charity throughout his lifetime. The money came from proceeds from his Newman's Own food line that he cofounded with writer A. E. Hotchner in 1982. The products started with salad dressing and grew to include more than 150 varieties of all-natural food and beverage products. Pasta sauce, salsa, popcorn, and lemonade are just a few of the products made.

In 1988, Newman cofounded the Hole in the Wall Gang Camp in Ashford, Connecticut. It is a residential summer camp free for children with cancer or other serious illnesses. The camp now has locations in the United States, Ireland, France, and Israel. About 13,000 children attend each year.

Final Days

In 2008, Newman was planning to direct a Connecticut stage production of John Steinbeck's *Of Mice and Men*. In May, however, he gave up his duties because of his declining health. In June, news sources reported that Newman had been diagnosed with lung cancer. He was being treated with chemotherapy at Memorial Sloan-Kettering Hospital in New York City. In August, Newman returned to his Westport, Connecticut, home, where

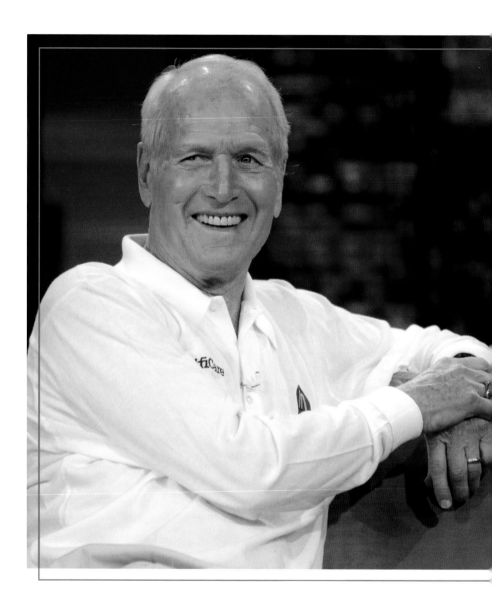

he died on September 26, 2008. He was surrounded by family and close friends. Newman was 83.

Throughout his career, Newman often played the role of the rebel.

Hud received seven Oscar nominations.

An Overview of *Hud*

Hud is a modern-day Western starring Newman as Hud Bannon, an immoral troublemaker who does not care what people think. This 1963 black-and-white film was inspired by the book *Horseman, Pass By*, published in 1961 and written by Pulitzer Prize–winning author Larry McMurtry.

Homer and Hud Bannon

Hud takes place on Homer Bannon's Texas cattle ranch. Homer is a lawful man with strong principles—a moral patriarch of his community. Throughout the story, he is in constant conflict with Hud, his grown son who lives on the ranch. Hud is a self-centered heavy drinker who arrogantly parks his pink Cadillac convertible outside married women's houses. He boasts, "The only question I ever ask any woman is, 'What time is your husband coming home?'"[1] Hud claims that if "you don't look out for yourself, the only helping hand you'll ever get is when they lower the box."[2]

Hud is especially brutal toward his father. He constantly criticizes how his father runs the ranch. Hud makes fun of him for standing by ethical principles. Homer, on the other hand, does not hesitate to criticize his son's shameful actions and playboy lifestyle. He also holds Hud responsible for the car accident that resulted in the death of Hud's older brother. Homer tells his son, "You're an unprincipled man, Hud. . . . You don't value nothin'. You don't respect nothin'. You live just for yourself. And that makes you not fit to live with."[3]

Lon and Alma

In spite of Hud's lack of morality, he is the story's main character. Although characters in the film are repulsed by Hud and his activities, many of them are still drawn to his good looks, charm, and recklessness. Lon Bannon, Hud's 17-year-old nephew and son of his deceased brother, is especially drawn to him. Hud tries to discourage Lon from worshipping and adoring him, but Lon insists on following his uncle's example. Lon is captivated by Hud, who has no boundaries.

Lon is torn between following his wild uncle or his decent grandfather. When Lon chooses to follow Hud, and even defend him, Homer says to his grandson, "Little by little, the look of the country changes because of the men we admire. You're just going to have to make up your own mind one day about what's right and wrong."[4]

Men have the dominant roles in *Hud*. There are a few women who appear in bars or have illicit affairs with Hud. There is only one significant female role: Alma Brown. Alma is the kind, down-to-earth housekeeper who lives in a small cabin on the ranch. Homer Bannon, a widower, employs Alma, a divorcée in her early thirties, to clean, cook, and shop. Alma is both disgusted by and attracted to Hud. However, she realizes that a man like Hud should be kept at a distance.

The Fate of the Ranch

The conflict in the story revolves around a disease that has spread through the ranch's cattle herd. The cattle have hoof-and-mouth disease, a highly contagious virus that is sometimes fatal. According to the law, animals with the disease must be destroyed. Hud wants to sell the cattle and reap the profits before government inspectors discover they are diseased. But Homer replies indignantly, "That would run the risk of starting an epidemic." Hud has no scruples and shouts at his father, "You gonna let them shoot your cows out from under you on account of a schoolbook disease?"[5] He continues his tirade by accusing the government of benefiting from epidemics.

Hud wants out of the ranch, and he wants his part of the profits. Homer rejects his son's unethical suggestion to sell the cattle and makes plans to kill the herd. In a disturbing scene, the ranch hands use huge tractors to dig a deep pit on the property. Then hundreds of noisy cattle are forced into the pit, where they are shot and killed. The men, dressed in rubber and plastic from head to toe, ceremoniously sprinkle the dead cows with lye. The substance will eventually liquefy the carcasses. The scene ends with the tractors pushing soil back into the pit.

There seems to be no end to Hud's callousness. Angry and violent, he becomes extremely drunk,

Newman, *left,* and Melvyn Douglas as Homer in a scene from *Hud*

barges into Alma's cabin, and tries to rape her. Hearing the commotion, Lon bursts in and pulls Hud from Alma. Lon clearly believes that Hud has gone too far, and he walks away from his uncle in disgust. Alma immediately packs her bags and leaves the ranch. Even when his father has a fatal heart attack, Hud's character does not soften.

The film ends as Hud enters the ranch house. He goes to the refrigerator, gets a beer, and opens it. He then goes to close the door to the house. With a smile on his face, Hud reminds the audience that he has not changed.

Patricia Neal received an Oscar for Best Actress for her role as Alma in *Hud*.

How to Apply Historical Criticism to *Hud*

What Is Historical Criticism?

Some forms of criticism draw from external notions to help analyze the work's meaning. Historical criticism is one example of this. It looks at the historical and social circumstances of the time in which the work was created. It analyzes how the historical occurrences and social surroundings of a film influence the film itself, and how a film can be seen as a reflection of its historical place or as a reaction to current events and other things occurring at the time it was created.

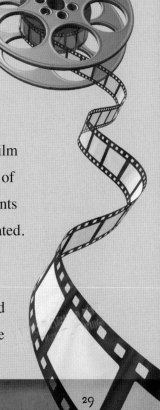

Applying Historical Criticism to *Hud*

Beginning in 1930, Hollywood was governed by the Motion Picture Production Code. It set the

standard for what was morally acceptable in motion pictures. Among the guiding principles was, "No picture shall be produced which will lower the moral standards of those who see it. Hence the sympathy of the audience shall never be thrown to the side of crime, wrong-doing, evil or sin."[1] In addition, movies were not to present adultery, rape, or alcohol abuse in a positive light. However, by the 1960s, social rules rendered these standards obsolete. According to one writer, *Hud* was "one of the first movies to show a bad guy making good."[2] *Hud, which was released in 1963, represents Hollywood's turn to new social standards. Hud rejects former industry guidelines by showing behavior that had formerly been unacceptable (such as alcoholism, adultery, and rebellion against the law) can go unpunished and that villains are not always unlikable.*

The audience is immediately introduced to Hud's reputation before they even lay eyes on

---

Thesis Statement

The thesis statement in this critique is: "*Hud*, which was released in 1963, represents Hollywood's turn to new social standards. *Hud* rejects former industry guidelines by showing behavior that had formerly been unacceptable (such as alcoholism, adultery, and rebellion against the law) can go unpunished and that villains are not always unlikable." The thesis answers the question: How was *Hud* a reflection of the historical period in which it was created? This thesis argues that *Hud* reflects changing social values.

the character. <u>Hud is a drinker,
brawler, and womanizer who
openly defies traditional values.</u>
The movie opens with Hud's
17-year-old nephew, Lon, in
search of his uncle. Lon notices
the bar owner sweeping up
broken glass outside his front
door and comments, "Must've
had quite a brawl in here last
night." The barkeep responds by
saying, "I had Hud in here last
night is what I had." Unsurprised by the news, Lon
replies, "It sure looks it."[3] The young man is neither
shocked nor disgusted when he hears of his uncle's
carousing the night before.

> **Argument One**
>
> The author has started to argue her thesis. Her first point is: "Hud is a drinker, brawler, and womanizer who openly defies traditional values." The author will offer many instances from the film as evidence to support this claim. She is contrasting Hud's rebellious behavior with the more traditional behavior of his father, Homer.

Lon finds his uncle's car parked outside the
house of a married woman and honks the horn to
summon Hud. As the two prepare to leave, the
woman's husband, Joe, pulls up. He demands,
"Which one of you two is coming out of my house
at 6:30 in the morning?" It is evident that Hud
knows how to fast-talk his way out of trouble. He
replies that it was his "snot-nose nephew," and
assures Joe that he will take care to dole out some

punishment "behind the woodshed."[4] When Lon criticizes Hud for casting the blame on him, Hud tells him to relax and jokes that once the story gets out, it will only boost Lon's reputation. Hud's blatant lack of remorse and his ability to laugh off his affair are evidence of his complete lack of respect for traditional values. He places more value on a lewd reputation than on upright actions.

Throughout the movie, Hud drinks heavily and is frequently disrespectful to his aging father. He carries on affairs with married women and then flaunts his relationships with them. He knows his father disapproves, but he does not care at all for the man's principles, which he perceives to be outdated. Hud's character reflects the changing attitude toward sex outside of marriage, as well as a diminishing respect for authority.

By 1963, America was shedding some of the straightlaced principles that had defined the 1940s and the 1950s. Society was beginning to drift away from a moral code concerned with the community's judgment of a person's actions and instead edged toward self-satisfaction, which would come into full bloom in the late 1960s.

Hud exemplifies the self-indulgence that was becoming more common when the film was created. The day after the movie debuted, *New York Times* movie reviewer Bosley Crowther wrote, "This heel, named Hud, is a rancher who is fully and foully diseased with all the germs of materialism that are infecting and sickening modern man. He is a nineteen-sixties specimen of the I'm-gonna-get-mine breed—the selfish, snarling smoothie who doesn't give a hoot for anyone else."[5]

> **Argument Two**
> The author now offers her second point: "*Hud* exemplifies the self-indulgence that was becoming more common when the film was created." She has started to show how Hud's behavior is a reflection of the values of American society in the 1960s.

The lowest point Hud seems to hit is on the night he becomes drunk and attempts to rape Alma. At that point, Alma chooses to leave the ranch. Unlike Hud, she still maintains some of the traditional principles, evident when she instructs Lon, "You look after your grandpa. He's getting old and feeble. He's your job now."[6] She adds that he should not be lazy. Alma and Homer take pride in a hard day's work, unlike Hud, who is happier to meet up with the next woman in town rather than work on the ranch.

Hud's quest for self-satisfaction and his open questioning of authority seem to parallel those attitudes in society. In the 1960s at colleges across the country, students were encouraged to question authority. This decade saw protests, sit-ins, and marches in the name of causes such as civil rights, the antiwar movement, and the feminist movement. Many viewed breaking the law in the name of their cause as commendable.

Upon hearing that a government agency might demand the whole cattle herd be destroyed if test results reveal a contagious disease, Hud immediately rails against the laws demanding extermination of the diseased cattle. He knows that voluntary destruction of the herd will result in severe economic hardship for the ranch. By trying to convince his father to sell off the cattle before test results reveal whether the animals are infected, he demonstrates that he is not concerned with the greater good, even though it could cause an epidemic throughout the cattle of the region. He argues that his father is allowing a government agent to come in and run his business. Like the young generation of the 1960s, Hud questions the government's right to enforce such a law.

Hud Bannon, *right*, is a heavy drinker whose actions influence his nephew, Lon.

He believes it is better to break the law than to suffer the consequences of abiding by it.

By the end of the movie, Hud is spared the usual consequences other previous film villains faced. He does not end up in jail, die, or have to answer to the husbands of the married women with whom he has carried on affairs.

Earlier in the film he shares his cold, cynical view on death with Lon when he says, "Happens to everybody: horses, dogs, men. Nobody

Argument Three

The author has argued that Hud's behavior is self-indulgent and rebellious. She is now addressing the second part of her thesis. She states, "By the end of the movie, Hud is spared the usual consequences other previous film villains faced." The author is arguing that the lack of consequences that Hud's character suffers is a commentary on the society's values at the time: that bad behavior can go unpunished.

gets out of life alive."[7] When his father dies in his arms, Hud is not even brought to tears. He is thoroughly unrepentant for his actions throughout the movie, and in the end, he gains control of the ranch. Despite his father's traditional belief that working cattle is respectable and honest work, Hud intends to drill for oil. To the end, his interests are in seeking personal gain and an easier life.

Although Hud is a selfish character intent on pursuing "loose living," movie audiences liked him. No longer were movie villains entirely despicable. This reflects changing social norms about right and wrong in the 1960s. Hud was intended to be a villain, so Newman was surprised to discover that young people were hanging up *Hud* posters and viewing his character as a hero—a new villainous brand for the radical social climate of the film's era.

Conclusion

This final paragraph is the conclusion of the critique. The author sums up her arguments and offers additional information about how the film was received. By telling the reader that movie audiences admired Hud, the villain of the film, she further reinforces her thesis statement.

Thinking Critically about *Hud*

Now it's your turn to assess the critique. Consider these questions:

1. The thesis statement answers the question of how *Hud* was a representation of the 1960s. What are some other ways to answer this question? Are there other questions you could address using historical criticism? How would you answer them?

2. Do you agree with the arguments used to support the thesis statement? Would you use any other elements from the film to support the thesis? What was the most interesting claim made?

3. This conclusion offers additional information about how audiences received the film. Does this information change the way you think about the film? Who do you think has the power to determine whether a character is a hero or a villain: the writer, the actor, or the audience?

Other Approaches

What you have just read is one possible way to apply historical criticism to *Hud,* but other writers have approached the film in different ways. Historical criticism takes into account the events happening at the time in which a film was produced. Following are two alternate approaches.

Analyzing the Outcome

Other writers have argued that, despite Homer's ultimate death, traditional values win in the end. Hud's father consistently condemns Hud's behavior and obeys the law by destroying the herd of diseased cattle. Hud's young nephew, who represents the "next" generation, is torn between what to idolize: traditional values or new radical values. He ultimately chooses to leave Hud, symbolically choosing to follow traditional moral standards of right and wrong. Additionally, although Alma is divorced and admits to having affairs with men, her strong work ethic and principles are more like Homer's than Hud's.

A thesis statement for such a critique could be: Through the characters of Homer, Lon, and Alma,

Hud makes the statement that society can overcome villainy.

Hud as a Comment on Materialism

When the film *Hud* was released in 1963, *New York Times* movie reviewer Bosley Crowther labeled Hud as the epitome of a materialistic and greedy culture. Hud is out to make an easy dollar by drilling for oil and living off the income. He sets out for personal gain and an easier life. His father, Homer, resents these qualities in his son.

A thesis statement for a critique that discusses materialism might be: By portraying Hud negatively and Homer positively, the filmmakers contrast hard work with laziness—and in doing so, they condemn greed.

Cool Hand Luke was released in 1967.

5

An Overview of
Cool Hand Luke

Cool Hand Luke is based on the 1965
novel of the same name written by Donn
Pearce. In 1949 at the age of 20, Pearce,
a talented safecracker, was arrested
for burglary. He served two years in a
Florida prison, working on chain gangs.
Pearce was an advisor for the film and
appeared briefly in the movie as a convict named
Sailor. The film was nominated for four Academy
Awards. It won only one for Best Supporting Actor.
(George Kennedy as Dragline).

Conviction

In the film *Cool Hand Luke*, Lucas "Luke"
Jackson, played by Newman, is incarcerated in a
Southern prison for the crime of cutting off the tops

of two long rows of parking meters. He did not take the money out of them, though. He just slowly cut them with a pipe cutter, let them fall to the ground, and paused from time to time to drink from his bottle of hard liquor. When the police arrived, he did not resist arrest. He just smiled.

Luke is convicted of "maliciously destroying municipal property while under the influence" and ends up in prison.[1] Every day, Luke does grueling roadwork on his chain gang—Road Prison 36—with 49 other prisoners. Under the searing sun, they chop weeds by the side of the road and shovel gravel on top of freshly spread tar. They ask permission of one of the bosses before making any moves. After an official nod, they can remove their shirts or hats.

Prison Life

The rules are made clear from the time Luke first arrives: Don't lose your spoon, everyone in their bunks by eight o'clock, and no fighting allowed in the building—only outside on Saturday afternoons. Punishment is the same for all infractions: a night in the box—a tiny wooden hut with no windows and a secure lock on the outside.

Luke spends plenty of nights in the box. He refuses to be bound by prison rules. Luke also changes the definition of winning. Every time he loses, he comes out a winner—a hero in the eyes of the prisoners. In a Saturday afternoon fight, fellow prisoner Dragline beats Luke brutally. But Luke won't give up, getting up repeatedly just to be beaten down again. Luke's suffering becomes the focus of the fight, and the other prisoners begin cheering for Luke, the underdog. By not giving up, Luke actually "wins" the fight and gains the respect of the prisoners, including Dragline.

That night, Luke comes out a hero again, this time in a poker game. With his laid-back style and poker face, Luke bluffs his opponent with a handful of nothing. Dragline proclaims to the loser, "He beat you with nothin'. Just like today, when he just kept comin' back at me, with nothin'."[2] Luke responds, "Yeah, well, sometimes nothin' can be a real cool hand."[3] And thus Luke earns his nickname, Cool Hand Luke.

Luke again proves he is a winner in a memorable scene with 50 eggs. Luke bets the other men he can eat 50 hard-boiled eggs in an hour, without throwing up, and the men eventually bet all their money that he cannot. When Luke succeeds in eating the eggs, he walks away with every cent in the bunkhouse.

Rebellion and Escape

When Luke's mother dies, the Captain puts him in the box to keep him from running away to his mother's funeral. The prisoners sympathize with Luke; after all, he has done nothing wrong. After his mother is buried, Luke goes back to the bunkhouse. But he can no longer tolerate being locked up, and he rebels. He cuts a hole in the wooden floor and escapes while the other inmates distract the guards. When the guard counts 49 instead of 50 prisoners, the bloodhounds are sent out to find Luke. He confuses the dogs by running through water, crossing land on overhead wires, and leaping over fences. Luke is finally captured, with a smirk on his face, and returned to prison. But in losing, he wins again—one of the bloodhounds is dead.

The Captain, a guard with a distinctive squeaky voice, now steps up his discipline of his most rebellious prisoner. He puts Luke in chains and makes him an example to the rest of the men. In one of the film's most memorable lines, the

Captain says, "What we've got here is failure to communicate. Some men you just can't reach."[4]

Luke escapes a second time, in his chains, and again confounds the bloodhounds by sprinkling cayenne pepper on a bridge. While Luke is gone,

Cool Hand Luke breaks rules and does not conform.

the inmates admit that prison is boring without him. He has almost become their reason for existing. When Luke is captured again, he tells the other prisoners, "Stop feedin' off me!"[5] But his endless determination and defiance only make him larger and larger in the eyes of his fellow prisoners. The more severe his punishment, the more they respect him.

A Clever Trick

After one relentless night of punishment, Luke appears to reach the breaking point. He begs the boss not to hit him anymore. He wraps his arms around the boss's ankle and promises he will never run again. He becomes the model prisoner, conforming to the rules and turning into the boss's favorite. The other prisoners do not like Luke anymore and turn against him. He is no longer their hero. But it is all a sham. Luke's favor with the boss gains him access to the keys to the trucks. He speeds away in one of them, with the keys to the other trucks in his pocket. Dragline manages to jump on the running board and escape with him. "You're an original, that's what you are," Dragline tells Luke.[6]

When Luke is finally captured, he shoots off the famous line to the main boss, the one whose eyes the audience never sees behind his reflective sunglasses: "What we got here is failure to communicate."[7] The boss then shoots Luke in the neck. Dragline carries his wounded friend to the sheriff's car and then violently attacks the boss, knocking off his sunglasses. As the sheriff's car leaves, Luke's head falls to one side, his mouth curved slightly in a smirk. The car then runs over the sunglasses. Just when the viewer thinks Luke has finally lost, Luke emerges a winner once again.

Back at the prison, Luke has already become a legend. Dragline tells the inmates, "He was smilin' . . . that's right. You know, that, that Luke smile of his. He had it on his face right to the very end. . . . he was some boy . . . a natural-born world-shaker."[8]

Newman stars as the antihero in *Cool Hand Luke*.

How to Apply Archetypal Criticism to *Cool Hand Luke*

What Is Archetypal Criticism?

Archetypal criticism evaluates a work through a main character or a central idea with which most people can identify. An archetype is a symbol that recurs often enough in real life or in literature to make it recognizable by most people. A reader or a viewer can easily relate to these common symbolic individuals or themes.

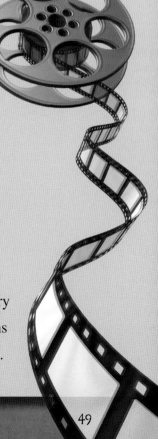

Swiss psychiatrist Carl Jung proposed that behind every person lies the collective typical experience of the human race. He called it the "collective unconscious"—a huge storehouse of the mind filled with human experience. His theory suggests that everyone can identify with emotions and patterns of behavior that all humanity shares.

Literary critic Northrop Frye taught that archetypal criticism could help explain a reader's experience and expand our understanding of how fiction works.

Some of the more familiar archetypal characters are the hero, the trickster, the nonconformist, the underdog, and the mother or father figure. There are also the martyr, the king, the devil, the magician, the goddess, and Christ the Messiah. Their familiar characteristics and actions are well known to readers or audiences. Some archetypes are ideas such as birth, death, harvest, seasons, fear, or loss. The reader or the viewer connects with these people or ideas and shares emotionally in their experiences.

Critiquing *Cool Hand Luke*

The hero of the 1967 film *Cool Hand Luke* is a nonconformist, a rebel, and a loner. A tagline for one of the film's posters reads, "The man . . . and the motion picture that simply do not conform."[1] The 1960s was a decade of nonconformity and protest against establishment. *Cool Hand Luke* fed the mindset of the era. Cool Hand Luke was a man who would not give up or give in, even though he was beaten and insulted. He was also willing to die for his beliefs and for his friends. Viewers identified with Luke and saw the admirable aspects of his character.

Throughout the film, visual and plot clues make it clear to the viewers that Cool Hand Luke is a Christ archetype. This serves to reinforce the idea that Luke must die, but that his legacy will live on after his death.

Director Stuart Rosenberg repeatedly weaves religious references and parallels to Christ through the entire story line. He creates numerous visual images of a modern-day Christ figure. Some critics claim that Luke's fellow inmates are like disciples who support and follow him. The most apparent allusion to a Christ figure comes after one of the film's most comical scenes. Luke is determined to prove he can eat 50 hard-boiled eggs without throwing up. He sits with a towel draped over his head, similar to the common image of

---

Thesis Statement

The thesis statement in this critique is: "Throughout the film, visual and plot clues make it clear to the viewers that Cool Hand Luke is a Christ archetype. This serves to reinforce the idea that Luke must die, but that his legacy will live on after his death." The author connects Luke to the Christ archetype and further explains that this connection emphasizes the themes of death and legacy.

Argument One

The author has started to argue her thesis. She asserts: "Director Stuart Rosenberg repeatedly weaves religious references and parallels to Christ through the entire story line." This addresses the first portion of her thesis, in which she connects Luke to the Christ archetype. She will offer examples to support this point.

Jesus with a shroud over his head. When Luke successfully eats 50 eggs, the prisoners lay him out on a table. His arms are stretched out, his head is tilted to the left, his eyes are closed, and his feet are crossed. The camera slowly moves above this scene, unmistakably associating Luke with the common depiction of Christ dying on the cross. It is a symbolic image familiar to most people.

Luke's lifestyle is very much the opposite of the life that Jesus Christ lived. Luke is arrested in a drunken stupor for destroying public property; Jesus Christ was arrested but had done nothing wrong. Luke is very outspoken and talks back to the prison guards; Jesus was silent before his accusers. Luke gambles, scams his opponents, steals a truck, and deceives the prison warden. He does not care much about his fellow inmates, although they adore him. Luke is bullheaded, irreverent, antisocial, and rebellious. Jesus, on the other hand, was kind to his enemies, loyal to his disciples, and devoted to doing good. The irony that Luke parallels Christ is

Argument Two

The author's second argument is: "The irony that Luke parallels Christ is a skillful technique of this film. It adds humor to the story with which most viewers can associate." The author is emphasizing the humor of the film, as well as showing how archetype theory helps the audience relate to a character in a film.

Luke eats 50 hard-boiled eggs in a memorable scene from *Cool Hand Luke*.

a skillful technique of this film. It adds humor to the story with which most viewers can associate.

Luke also parallels Jesus in his relationship with his mother. Luke's mother, Arletta, visits her son in prison. Luke says a final good-bye to her and then gives her over to the care of his brother John. Similarly, when Jesus was hanging on the cross, he gave the care of his mother, Mary, over to his disciple John, whom he

> **Argument Three**
> The author's third argument gives an example showing how Luke and Christ have similarities. She asserts: "Luke also parallels Jesus in his relationship with his mother."

loved dearly. This similarity is quite ironic. Luke's chain-smoking, rough-talking mother stands in stark contrast to Mary, whom God highly favored to be the mother of Jesus.

The film's climactic scene also has a strong religious analogy: It is reminiscent of Jesus praying in the garden of Gethsemane before he was arrested. The scene takes place in an abandoned country church where Luke is hiding from authorities after his third escape. Luke sits on a wooden pew and talks in monologue to God. He calls God "Ol' Man" and complains, "You ain't dealt me no cards in a long time. . . . What do ya got in mind for me?" Finally, he kneels down and prays, "On my knees, askin'."[2] In the garden of Gethsemane, Jesus also prayed, asking God to prevent his suffering but stating that He was willing to do God's will.

When police surround the church where Luke is hiding, Luke opens a window and gives the prison warden a clear shot at him. Luke is killed with a bullet to the neck, and the viewer recognizes he

> **Argument Four**
>
> The author continues to offer examples in her fourth point: "The film's climactic scene also has a strong religious analogy: It is reminiscent of Jesus praying in the garden of Gethsemane before he was arrested."

has died willingly and without a struggle—as a martyr and a hero. Jesus died a similar death by not resisting arrest and going willingly to the cross.

<u>Luke also is a Christlike figure because he is an underdog. Luke becomes a legend back at the prison, and it is implied that his story will live on.</u> Christ the Messiah was an unlikely hero with a humble upbringing and no political power. In many ways, Jesus and Luke were expected to lose. Luke is the likely loser throughout the entire film, but like Jesus, he never gives up. The death of Jesus on the cross appeared to be his end, but he rose from death three days later.

> **Argument Five**
> The author's final point highlights how the archetype in the film emphasizes themes of death and legacy. She states: "Luke also is a Christlike figure because he is an underdog. Luke becomes a legend back at the prison, and it is implied that his story will live on."

In *Cool Hand Luke*, the other prisoners, as well as the viewers, see Luke as a winner, even when he seems to lose. Luke loses the fistfight with Dragline but comes out a hero in the minds of his fellow prisoners. Luke bluffs all the inmates in a poker game, takes all their money, but earns their respect and the nickname "Cool Hand Luke."

In the final scene, Dragline is shown in chains, chopping weeds alongside a road. He is at a crossroads, and again, depicting a religious image, the camera angle emphasizes the resemblance of the crossroads to a crucifix. Over the scene is superimposed a photograph of Cool Hand Luke. The photograph has crease lines in the shape of a cross.

Cool Hand Luke is the archetype of Christ. He uses his intelligence to get what he wants, is willing to sacrifice himself, and manages to win even when he loses. By highlighting the Christ archetype, the filmmakers give the audience a foreshadowing of what is to come—that ultimately, Cool Hand Luke would be killed for his radical nonconformity.

> **Conclusion**
> The last paragraph is the conclusion. The author has made her arguments, and now reiterates her thesis statement. This conclusion highlights the usefulness of using archetypes in film: By connecting a character to a well-known archetype, the filmmakers have allowed audiences to identify with the character portrayed on-screen.

Thinking Critically about *Cool Hand Luke*

Now it's your turn to assess the critique.
Consider these questions:

1. The thesis statement identifies Luke with the Christ archetype. Do you agree with this? Can you think of any arguments to refute this?

2. What was the most interesting argument made? What other plot or character elements could be used to support the thesis?

3. Can you think of any other archetypes that might exist in the film *Cool Hand Luke*? What are they? What evidence from the film would you use to support those archetypes?

Other Approaches

What you have just read is one possible way to apply archetypal criticism to *Cool Hand Luke*. Other writers and experts have approached it in different ways. Archetypal criticism seeks to relate characters to other well-known characters or symbols. Following are two additional approaches.

Cool Hand Luke as an Antihero

Although Luke's life contains parallels to the life of Christ, a critic might choose to emphasize Luke's negative qualities as a protagonist. One common archetype in literature and film is the antihero—a person who defies the traditional characteristics of a hero but who ultimately succeeds in his own way. In some cases, an antihero can actually be villainous.

Film critic Roger Ebert describes how Cool Hand Luke portrays an antihero. He writes, "[It] used to be the anti-hero was a bad guy we secretly liked. Then . . . we got a bad guy we didn't like. And now, in 'Cool Hand Luke,' we get a good guy who becomes a bad guy because he doesn't like us."[3] Ebert writes that Luke understood himself so well that he could tell the other characters and the audience "to shove off."[4]

The thesis statement for a critique that examines Luke as an antihero might be: Unlike traditional heroes, Luke is a rule-breaking criminal who ultimately gains the admiration of those around him—and the admiration of the audience.

Arguing against the Christ Archetype

Another way to approach *Cool Hand Luke* using archetype theory would be to argue against applying the Christ archetype to Luke's character. Author Elena Oumano called Luke the "convict Christ."[5] Instead of claiming that parallels do not exist, the essay could show that the obvious comparison was a tool for irony in the film.

A thesis statement for such a critique might be: The very concept of Luke as a convict Christ creates an irony that overshadows any serious parallels between Luke and Christ. But this irony allows for humor by giving the audience a well-known archetype (Christ) to which they can compare Luke.

Essential Critiques

Robert Redford starred with Newman in *Butch Cassidy and the Sundance Kid*.

An Overview of *Butch Cassidy and the Sundance Kid*

Butch Cassidy and the Sundance Kid is a tale of the Old West in the 1890s. The film includes lots of action, comedy, drama, and romance. Newman, the main character, dubbed it "an adult fairy tale."[1]

   Butch Cassidy and the Sundance Kid is part of a genre of movies named buddy films. A buddy film has two equally important male protagonists who are inseparable friends. They have their differences, but their loyalty to each other is limitless. The two buddies in *Butch Cassidy* are Butch Cassidy, played by Newman, and the Sundance Kid, played by Robert Redford.

   Newman played the part of Butch Cassidy, a polite, gentlemanly outlaw who is nearly impossible not to like. He is the brains, and the one who knows how to get his way, usually through clever negotiation. Sundance tells him, "You just keep thinkin', Butch. That's what you're good at."[2] Butch responds boastfully, "Boy, I got vision, and the rest of the world wears bifocals."[3]

The Likable Outlaws

The film divides neatly into three sections: Butch and Sundance's unlawful escapades, the chase, and their Bolivian adventure. In the first section, the viewer gets to know Butch and Sundance, as well as Sundance's girlfriend, Etta Place. Etta seems to like both of them, and they both seem to like her. The audience learns that Butch is the leader of a gang of outlaws called the Hole in the Wall Gang. There is no one who can strip him of that position. The viewer also discovers that Butch would rather rob banks than trains, because "they don't move."[4] He also lets the audience know that he wants to enlist in the Army and fight in the Spanish-American War.

The pair's main targets are trains owned by the Union Pacific Railroad. With the gang's vast supply of dynamite, they could easily blow up the trains. But Butch politely asks passengers for all their valuables. He also negotiates with railroad employees to open the safe on the train. Woodcock, the frightened keeper of the railroad's money, timidly tells Butch in one scene, "Ah, Butch, you know that if it were my money, there is nobody that I would rather have steal it than you."[5] But he went on to emphasize that he was protecting the railroad's money at all costs.

In spite of Butch and Sundance's manners, everyone is afraid of them. The sheriff cannot get anyone to volunteer for a posse to go after them and the other members of their gang. Eventually, six of the best lawmen in the country relentlessly track Butch and Sundance. The two men never see the faces of their pursuers. The only thing they see is the white straw hat that one of them always wears. Butch and Sundance narrowly avoid being caught on more than one occasion. Sundance says, "Hey, Butch, they're very good."[6] Butch has never been outsmarted so many times, and he repeatedly asks, "Who *are* those guys?"[7] The long pursuit culminates with Butch and Sundance jumping off a high cliff to escape into the raging waters of a river.

Going Out with a Bang

Soon Butch, Sundance, and Etta are living the high life in New York City. Then they board a ship and sail to Bolivia. Sundance is angry that they have stepped into a land of poverty. Butch replies, "It could be worse. You get a lot more for your money in Bolivia. . . ."[8] He adds that Sundance will feel a lot better after he's robbed a couple of banks. And that's just what they do.

Etta teaches them just enough Spanish so they can hold up banks. They learn how to say phrases such as, "This is a robbery," "All of you back against the wall," and "Give me the money."[9] But their thievery draws out the Bolivian police, who pursue them relentlessly, although unsuccessfully. In one scene, Butch spots the man with the white straw hat. As tension mounts and the captors close in, Etta decides to return home. She's had enough and doesn't want to see Butch and Sundance get killed.

In the last scene, a young stable boy turns in the two outlaws when he spots a donkey they stole. Hundreds of lawmen converge on the small town where Butch and Sundance are passing through. Butch and Sundance are both shot in the torso, but

the two still do not give up. Trapped in an empty
shed, Butch says to Sundance, "I've got a great idea
where we should go next. . . . Australia."[10] The men
run out shooting and into a barrage of gunfire.

Katharine
Ross played
Sundance's
girlfriend, Etta
Place.

The movie ends with a sepia-colored still shot
of Butch and Sundance running toward an army of
police. They are firing their guns and still alive. The
audience knows the pair does not have a chance.
But the film fittingly captures them as living myths
that will endure.

Butch Cassidy and the Sundance Kid became the most popular film of 1969 and won four Academy Awards.

How to Apply Gender Criticism to *Butch Cassidy and the Sundance Kid*

What Is Gender Criticism?

Gender criticism explores how an artistic work conveys ideas about men and women. This approach seeks to understand how the creative piece depicts what is masculine and what is feminine. Gender criticism considers how each gender is portrayed by characters, how they interact, and how they are perceived. Gender criticism broadly analyzes the work to consider how the piece's depiction of what is masculine and feminine reflects society's notions of gender.

Critiquing *Butch Cassidy and the Sundance Kid*

Butch Cassidy and the Sundance Kid has been labeled a quintessential "buddy movie." Paul

Newman and Redford are two outlaw robbers who are loyal to the end. Common male bandit stereotypes in film show men as violent, selfish, and willing to turn on a friend at the prospect of personal gain. In contrast to common stereotypes, the male characters in *Butch Cassidy and the Sundance Kid*—although outlaws—display loyalty, respectability, and friendship.

From the outset of the movie, the audience realizes that Butch and Sundance differ from many outlaw stereotypes. The two are gentleman outlaws who are not obsessed with violence. In an early scene, Sundance is accused of cheating at a game of poker. He is offended by the comment and tells Butch that if the accuser asks Sundance to stick around and play more poker, then he'll be willing to get up and leave. Butch congenially tries to talk the accuser into simply asking his partner and him to stay, but to no avail. He then turns to Sundance and says, "I can't help you, Sundance."[1] This seemingly innocent comment is Butch's subtle warning. When the poker player realizes he has just accused the Sundance Kid of cheating, he immediately explains, "I didn't know you were the Sundance Kid when I said you were cheating. If I draw on you, you'll kill me."[2] Butch senses the poker player knows he's in a tight spot and kindly reoffers him the chance to invite them to stay. He does.

As Butch and Sundance are leaving, the poker player asks Sundance how good he is. Sundance quick draws on him, shoots his holster off his body, and fires repetitive shots at the poker player's revolver, shooting it into a corner. Sundance leaves the man alive (and in awe) and walks out the door.

In other Westerns, such an accusation at the poker table would have resulted in a showdown or a brawl. But Butch and Sundance are content to leave the scene with no blood spilled. They do not display the mean tempers, touchy egos, and brutality that many male villains possess in Westerns.

During the movie's first train robbery, Sundance hops the train and demands that the conductor stop the train. One of the engine crewmen looks ahead, sees Butch standing next to the tracks, and excitedly exclaims, "That's old Butch himself!"[3] The outlaw's reputation does not frighten his victims, but rather, they are excited to meet the legendary outlaw. When the train comes to a stop, the crewman hops down. Sundance whirls toward him, and the man explains, "Well, I just thought I'd watch," showing no fear whatsoever of these affable train robbers.[4]

The two outlaws are perceived to be respectable by those around them—even those whom they rob. Woodcock, the frightened keeper of the railroad's money, timidly tells Butch in one scene, "If it were my money, there is nobody that I would rather have steal it than you." Instead of earning fear by acts of terror, their behavior seems to earn them respect because of how they treat their "victims."

Argument Two

The author now argues that Butch and Sundance are respectable characters. She states: "The two outlaws are perceived to be respectable by those around them—even those whom they rob." This adds a nuance to the previous argument by showing how characters in the film react to Butch and Sundance.

When forced to blow open the door after trying to reason with Mr. Woodcock fails, Butch helps the injured Mr. Woodcock, making sure he is not too badly hurt following the explosion.

<u>Throughout the film, Butch and Sundance treat females with respect and dignity.</u> The saloon girls have very small roles in the film, leaving Etta Place as the only female character of substance. Although Etta and Sundance are romantically involved, she and Butch are close friends as well. Both men enjoy her company and value what she can add to their small bank-robbing outfit.

> **Argument Three**
>
> Gender criticism takes into account how males treat females in a work. The author addresses this point in her next argument: "Throughout the film, Butch and Sundance treat females with respect and dignity."

When Butch and Sundance return to Etta's place after narrowly escaping being shot, Butch asks her whether she can feed them. She replies that she can and then tells him, "They said you were dead." Sundance replies with a surly, "Don't make a big thing out of it." But his gruff demeanor immediately crumbles. As she walks past, he changes his mind. "No. Make a big thing out of it," he says, and pulls her into a hug.[5] Sundance's soft, romantic side is a new characteristic for cowboy outlaws.

Later in the evening, when the men decide to pack up and head for Bolivia, they agree to ask Etta to join them. Sundance walks out to the porch where Etta is sitting. "I'll get you some more," she says, assuming they just want more food from her.[6] She has left the men alone to discuss "business," and since she is a woman, she does not imagine they would want to include her in their plan.

But Sundance tells her they have decided to ask her to come along. She speaks Spanish, and he acknowledges she could be useful. He says, "Butch speaks a little Spanish, and you speak it good. And it'd be good cover going with a woman. No one expects it. Then we could travel safer."[7]

In Bolivia, she sets out to teach Butch and Sundance enough Spanish so they can rob banks. She drills them night and day, while they are eating, and while they are in bed. The men respect her authority as their teacher and begrudgingly do their best to soak in the lessons.

The men are true friends and do not compete with each other. Butch is the brains of the operation, and Sundance is the phenomenal gunslinger. The men do not even allow any jealousy or rivalry over Etta to come between them. Butch keeps his relationship

> **Argument Four**
>
> In this point, the author is showing how Butch and Sundance are dissimilar to other Western outlaws who compete and argue with each other. She states: "The men are true friends and do not compete with each other."

with her strictly a friendship. Both men demonstrate trust and respect for one another. There are no accusations or jealous tirades, as one would expect in a Western. They complement one another instead of trying to outdo each other.

Sundance is loyal to Etta, and refers to her as "smart . . . and pretty . . . and sweet, and gentle, and tender, and refined and lovely and carefree,"

Butch and Sundance live their lives running from the law.

leading the audience to believe he values such qualities in a lady.[8] Unlike earlier Western villains, the men do not drink excessively or smoke. They are gentlemen.

Toward the end of the film, it is revealed that Butch has never killed anyone, and he is nervous at the prospect of having to do so. This is yet another example of how *Butch Cassidy and the Sundance Kid* broke the mold on male bandits.

By the end of the film, the duo has remained loyal. Neither turns in the other for reward money, and neither walks away from the partnership, despite being tracked by a posse of lawmen. Even to the end, the two are willing to die for one another. They remain true buddies, running headlong into their certain deaths side by side. Breaking the mold of stereotypical male bandits, neither Butch nor Sundance is willing to desert the other at any point in the movie. They might argue, but they play off each other humorously, even in trying situations. Their partnership is one of honor, respect, and loyalty.

Conclusion

The conclusion is the last paragraph of the critique. Here, the author reminds the reader that the two outlaws have remained loyal to one another: a mark of true friendship. She reiterates how these traits break the mold of stereotypical male outlaws.

Thinking Critically about *Butch Cassidy and the Sundance Kid*

Now it's your turn to assess the critique. Consider these questions:

1. The thesis statement makes a claim about what *Butch Cassidy and the Sundance Kid* tells us about males and females. Are there other questions you could ask using gender criticism? How would you answer them?

2. Do you agree with the arguments used to support the thesis statement? Which was the most convincing? What other elements from the plot could be used as support?

3. The author's conclusion claims that Butch and Sundance's friendship breaks common gender stereotypes about male bandits. Can you think of any other gender stereotypes that are either reinforced or refuted by the film's depiction of the men's friendship?

Other Approaches

You have just read one way to apply gender criticism to *Butch Cassidy and the Sundance Kid*. Other writers have looked at the film in different ways. Gender criticism looks at ways in which men and women are portrayed in a film. Following are two additional approaches.

Etta as a Complex Character

A common role for a female in a Western is the love interest of the main male character. Film reviewer James Berardinelli wrote that the director of *Sundance* "elevated the role of Etta Place from that of the traditional love interest to a more complex character."[9] A writer might use this review as a springboard to investigate how Etta continues the female role established in other Westerns, yet how her unique qualities benefit the outlaw gang.

A thesis statement for a critique that focuses on Etta's role might be: Etta as a character is similar to the civilizing previous female roles in Westerns. Yet here her femininity, as shown through her role as cook, teacher, and friend to the outlaws, draws out the softer side of the men around her and adds dimension to their gang.

Butch, Sundance, and Homosociality

The relationship between the two male protagonists in *Butch Cassidy and the Sundance Kid* is a good example of homosociality. Homosociality is defined as a nonsexual relationship between two people of the same gender. For men, homosocial relationships usually result in a close camaraderie. Eve Sedgwick researched homosocial representations in their link to homosexuality. She explains that homosocial[ity] "describes social bonds between persons of the same sex . . . and [is] meant to be distinguished from homosexual[ity]. In fact, it is applied to such activities as 'male bonding.'"[10] Butch and Sundance's relationship is one of homosociality. They enjoy each other's company, yet there is nothing sexual about their relationship. The presence of Etta and the few saloon girls Butch is involved with show the audience that their relationship is homosocial, and not homosexual, in nature.

One thesis statement for a critique that explores homosociality might be: Through its depiction of close male camaraderie, *Butch Cassidy and the Sundance Kid* explores homosociality as a social bond.

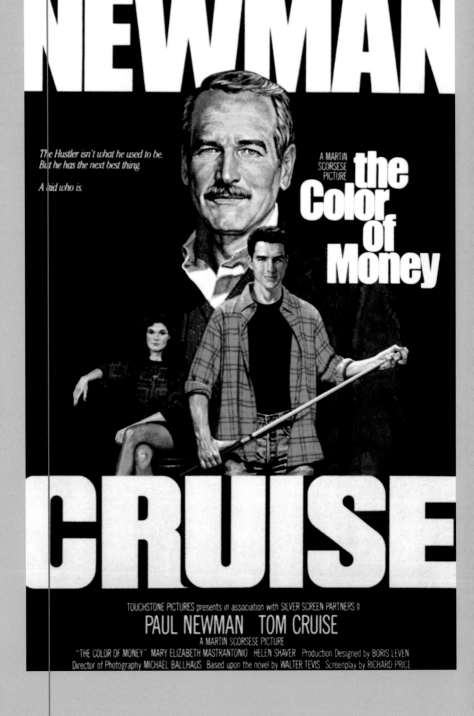

Martin Scorsese directed *The Color of Money.*

Chapter 9

An Overview of *The Color of Money*

The Color of Money (1986) as well as its prequel, *The Hustler* (1961), are based on novels by Walter Tevis. *The Color of Money* continues the story of pool shark Fast Eddie Felson where *The Hustler* left off. Newman starred as Eddie in both films. It has been 25 years since Eddie was banned from playing professional pool. Now middle-aged, Eddie Felson, a liquor salesman in Chicago, returns to teach a young toy store clerk, Vincent Lauria, how to hustle the game. Vincent is a rebellious hotshot who is trying to make a name for himself in local pool halls. Vincent reminds Eddie of himself, the pool player he was 25 years ago. Eddie sets out to make a fortune off Vincent and his girlfriend, Carmen.

HOLLYWOOD
PRODUCTION
DIRECTOR
CAMERA
DATE   SCENE

Eddie promises Vincent he can teach him how to play a smart game. He will show Vincent how to raise the stakes, hustle his opponent, and walk away with a bundle. All Eddie asks for is 60 percent of the take.

A New Protégé

Eddie is captivated the first time he sees Vincent play pool. But he is not just impressed with his game. He sees potential in the young man—the making of a hustler. Eddie calls him a "flake," the type of person whom other players will not take seriously. Eddie says that Vincent has the eye, the stroke, and the flake. Then Eddie begins to teach Vincent how to hustle, to trick his opponents into believing he can always be beaten.

Eddie persuades Vincent and Carmen to venture out on the road with him for six weeks. Vincent is eager to go and to win every game he plays. He proudly claims he is not going to lose often. Eddie says, "Oh yes you will. That's what I'm gonna teach ya. Sometimes if you lose, you win."[1]

Eddie is the brain; he controls when Vincent loses and when he wins a game of pool. They travel from city to city, from one shadowy pool hall to another. They stay in cheap motels and eat in dingy diners. And they hustle for the biggest pot of money.

It is important that Vincent be a good pool player, but not the best. He should not make a name for himself. Eddie says, "He should be the unknown. That would be nice. That would be beautiful. You could play around with that. You could control that."[2] Eddie has a hard time holding Vincent back from winning every game. Vincent complains to Eddie, "Why can't we have a hustle when I win?"[3] Eddie reminds Vincent he is the student and then says, "Because this is better than that. There's something at the end of this."[4] When the bets get higher and higher in favor of his opponent who has been winning, then Vincent is allowed to win and walk away with the money. Eddie calls it acting—it is a business and they are just trying to be professionals.

Eddie teaches Vincent to use the house cue sticks. If he brings in a nice cue stick, the other players will think he's good. Eddie tells him to play the lesser players first. If he beats the best players first, he will scare off everyone. Vincent does not always heed Eddie's advice, and the trio sometimes gets into trouble.

Confronting the Past

Eddie's goal is to end up in Atlantic City, New Jersey, for the 9-Ball Classic championship pool tournament. But Eddie is longing too much for the game—he wants to play pool himself and do his own hustling. When he can no longer hold himself back, Eddie returns to playing. However, his attempts to beat his opponents prove futile. He gets hustled by someone who plays like he used to play. Finally, Eddie hits rock bottom. Vincent attempts to console him, but Eddie lashes out. He sends Vincent and Carmen to Atlantic City by themselves.

After Vincent and Carmen leave, Eddie enthusiastically returns to the game. He does everything he can to restore his past and revitalize his game. He has his eyes checked, buys a pair of glasses, and practices seriously.

Eddie shows up in Atlantic City to play in the 9-Ball tournament himself. His spirit and his life seem renewed. Partway into the tournament, he is set up to play Vincent. Vincent misses a few shots, and Eddie wins. Eddie is thrilled.

Later, Vincent and Carmen show up at Eddie's door. They tell Eddie the game was rigged—that Vincent "dumped" the game—meaning he lost on

purpose. They give Eddie a share of the money Vincent won by dumping. Eddie is stunned.

Eddie forfeits his next game. He walks over to the stands, where Vincent and other spectators are viewing the tournament, and returns the money to Vincent. Eddie tells Vincent he wants to play him—without Vincent attempting to lose—and he is going to beat him. Eddie emphasizes he will keep playing Vincent until he wins. Vincent agrees to play, and asks him what makes him so sure he'll win. Eddie breaks and says, "Hey, I'm back."[5]

Vincent, who is played by Tom Cruise, learns all about hustling from Eddie.

Fast Eddie Felson is a former hustler who trains a young pool player in
The Color of Money.

How to Apply Psychoanalytic Criticism to *The Color of Money*

What Is Psychoanalytic Criticism?

Psychoanalytic criticism attempts to apply the concepts of psychoanalysis to literature, film, or other works. Psychoanalysis seeks to address issues such as repressed desires, dreams, or anxieties and to understand how they are affecting a person's conscious action. It holds that there are basic patterns of development that most people experience, and that these developmental patterns can be seen in certain characters.

Psychoanalytic criticism can evaluate a work by identifying and diagnosing the problems of a dysfunctional character. That character usually has an inner problem. Perhaps it is an unhealthy

social life or some sort of unacceptable behavioral pattern. The individual usually struggles with inner conflicts that need to be resolved. A psychoanalytic evaluation looks into a character's root problems and inner struggles and tries to understand them. It focuses on experiencing an individual's psyche, the center of the character's thoughts and emotions. The viewer may or may not choose to make conclusive judgments about the character.

Evaluating a movie through psychoanalysis can uncover overlooked themes—ideas that are overshadowed by lively action and plot. Discovering those themes is one of the intentions of psychoanalytic criticism.

Critiquing *The Color of Money*

Fast Eddie Felson, the main character in *The Color of Money*, is a fitting subject for psychoanalytic criticism. Eddie has several inner conflicts and behavioral problems that weave throughout the entire film. For 25 years, Eddie has been banned from playing professional pool, the one thing that had given him his identity and significance as a younger man. Eddie begins to train Vincent to be a hustler, just as he had been.

But eventually, Eddie's past catches up with him, and he wants success for himself, too. Eddie's longing to prove that he is not a has-been causes jealousy, competition, and Eddie's ultimate forfeit of the final pool match. Instead, he challenges Vincent to a match, refusing to stop until he has won. The psychology of this character displays unresolved and conflicted unconscious desires.

Eddie is typical of some older men who regret losing their former success. He tries to revive his past accomplishments by living vicariously through Vincent. Eddie was once one of the best pool sharks around and smart enough to make other players think they could beat him. But when he lost his ability to play the game of pool, he also lost his self-worth and self-esteem. Eddie reveals his

Thesis Statement

The thesis statement in this critique is: "Eddie's longing to prove that he is not a has-been causes jealousy, competition, and Eddie's ultimate forfeit of the final pool match. Instead, he challenges Vincent to a match, refusing to stop until he has won. The psychology of this character displays unresolved and conflicted unconscious desires." The thesis statement answers the question: How do Eddie Felson's unresolved desires influence his conscious actions?

Argument One

The author is now offering supporting points. Her first argument shows how Eddie fits into a category that helps the viewer understand why he acts like he does. She states: "Eddie is typical of some older men who regret losing their former success. He tries to revive his past accomplishments by living vicariously through Vincent."

inner conflict when he says, "Twenty-five years ago, I had the screws put on me. I mean, it was over for me before it really got started."[1] The viewer wonders for the rest of the movie whether Eddie will somehow regain his self-respect.

Eddie tries to resolve his inner struggles through Vincent, a young pool player with lots of talent. When Vincent plays pool, Eddie sees himself and tries to relive his life through this younger man who is so much like he used to be. Eddie decides to train Vincent to be not only a great pool player but also a great hustler, as he was. Eddie will make Vincent into himself, which is Eddie's way of feeling like a winner again and becoming significant. Eddie gives Vincent the credit for restoring his life and renewing his hope. He tells him, "I'm hungry again, and you've bled that back into me."[2]

Eddie enjoys being in the world of pool again, and he seems to like the feeling of self-assurance it gives him. But when it seems as if Eddie is coming to terms with himself, Eddie's unconscious jealousies and internal tensions cause

> **Argument Two**
>
> The author's second point shows how Eddie's unconscious desires cause tension in the plot of the film: "But when it seems as if Eddie is coming to terms with himself, Eddie's unconscious jealousies and internal tensions cause him to lash out against Vincent."

him to lash out against Vincent. Although Eddie's plan has been successful and the group has made money, small disputes arise when Vincent begins to question Eddie's authority. Vincent wonders why they cannot do things his way and why he cannot win all the time. Eventually, serious conflicts arise between the two men.

Mary Elizabeth Mastrantonio starred with Paul Newman and Tom Cruise.

Vincent does not do what Eddie tells him, and Eddie grows upset with his protégé. Vincent seems

Through Vincent, Eddie rediscovers his love of pool.

to love winning too much and is not willing to lose once in a while to deceive or hustle his opponent. It seems as if Eddie is jealous of Vincent, his own student whom he trained to be the best, perhaps because Vincent is a young, successful pool player, as Eddie once was. The viewer witnesses a complex power struggle between the two men as well as an insurmountable conflict in Eddie's own mind. Eddie wants Vincent to succeed, but mainly for Eddie's own fulfillment and as a way to make a lot of money at the game of pool.

Eddie spirals down into depression, drinking heavily, and losing at pool. He even gets tricked by another hustler who uses the same scam on Eddie that Eddie once used on other players. Vincent consoles Eddie after his loss, but Eddie lashes out and pushes Vincent away by giving him money and telling him to go to Atlantic City without him. Eddie tells Vincent that he has taught him all he needs to know, and that Vincent does not need him anymore. This action shows that Eddie's loss damaged his self-worth. Eddie seems embarrassed that his protégé witnessed his teacher's loss.

After Carmen and Vincent leave, Eddie cleans up and works on his game. At the 9-Ball Classic, it is clear that Eddie's very identity has become tied up with winning or losing. When he beats Vincent in the tournament, he is elated. As he leaves the pool hall, he even steps outside to celebrate for a few seconds before returning indoors. But when he finds out later that Vincent lost on purpose, it is clear that Eddie is distraught. He thought he had

> **Argument Three**
> The author's third argument claims a psychological reason for Eddie's action: "At the 9-Ball Classic, it is clear that Eddie's very identity has become tied up with winning or losing."

beaten his pupil fair and square. When he thought his win had been legitimate, he had been thrilled. Now he cannot move on without knowing he can beat Vincent. So he forfeits his tournament match and goes after Vincent with the intent to play him until he wins. Eddie is driven by his need to know that he can beat the best—his own pupil—in a fair game. The film ends before the viewer knows the outcome of the match between Eddie and Vincent, but Eddie's dialogue and enthusiasm seem to show that he is back in the game for good.

In *The Color of Money*, Eddie displays jealousy toward his young protégé. His actions are directly influenced by unresolved unconscious desires. He is caught between wanting Vincent's success and wanting his own success. He wants to rediscover his own identity. The plot ultimately centers on this personal battle that takes place in the mind and subconscious of Eddie as he revisits the very activity that had given him so much success and heartbreak in his younger years.

Conclusion
The final paragraph is the conclusion of the critique. The author reiterates her thesis and consolidates her arguments. She reminds the reader that Eddie's unconscious desires are influencing his actions.

Thinking Critically about *The Color of Money*

Now it's your turn to assess the critique.
Consider these questions:

1. The thesis statement answers the question of how unresolved desires affect the characters' conscious actions. Are there other questions you could ask using psychoanalytic criticism? How would you answer them?

2. What was the most interesting claim made? Can you think of any arguments against the thesis statement?

3. The concluding paragraph restates the thesis and the main arguments. It invites the reader to think critically about the topic. Do you agree that Eddie was motivated by unconscious desires? Why or why not?

Other Approaches

What you have just read is one way to apply psychoanalytic criticism to *The Color of Money*. Other experts have approached the film in different ways. Remember that psychoanalytic criticism attempts to apply the theories of psychoanalysis to the film. Following are two alternate approaches.

Eddie and the Role of Father

A critic might argue that, through his relationship with Vincent, Eddie has become a sort of father figure to the young pool player. In 2005, film critic Richard Schickel looked back nearly 20 years after *The Color of Money* was released. He wrote, "The movie ends with the old guy [Newman] and the Young Turk [Cruise], teacher and pupil, father figure and surrogate son . . . facing off in a national tournament."[3] While taking this relationship into account, one might argue that Eddie is less interested in self-worth, and instead driven by a desire to remind his "son" figure that he is still the best pool player—especially after Vincent witnessed Eddie's humiliating loss and "dumped" his own game against Eddie during the 9-Ball Classic.

A thesis statement for such a critique could be: As a self-interested father figure, Eddie is driven by a desire to prove to Vincent, the son figure, that he is still the better pool player.

Eddie and Defense Mechanisms

Sigmund Freud studied and put forth the idea of defense mechanisms. The theory states that the human mind has specific ways of managing anxieties that occur in life. These mechanisms include denial (refusing to accept obvious truth) and repression (forcing a painful event out of the mind). These mechanisms could be applied to Eddie to help describe his actions in the film. Eddie's attempts to deny and repress the memory of his traumatic banning from pool ultimately backfire. Reentering the game as Vincent's teacher forces him to acknowledge the emotions he had attempted to suppress—a desire for success as a hustler.

A thesis statement for such a critique might be: Eddie's failed attempts at denial and repression shape the conflict in *The Color of Money*. This thesis addresses the question: How do coping and defense mechanisms shape the narrative structure of the film?

You Critique It

Now that you have learned about several different critical theories and how to apply them to film, are you ready to perform a critique of your own? You have read that this type of evaluation can help you look at film from a new perspective and make you pay attention to certain issues you may not have otherwise recognized. So, why not use one of the critical theories profiled in this book to consider a fresh take on your favorite movie?

First, choose a theory and the movie you want to analyze. Remember that the theory is a springboard for asking questions about the work.

Next, write a specific question that relates to the theory you have selected. Then you can form your thesis, which should provide the answer to that question. Your thesis is the most important part of your critique and offers an argument about the work based on the tenets, or beliefs, of the theory you are applying. Recall that the thesis statement typically appears at the very end of the introductory paragraph of your essay. It is usually only one sentence long.

After you have written your thesis, find evidence to back it up. Good places to start are in the work itself or journals or articles that discuss what other people have said about it. You may also want to read about the screenwriter's or actors' lives so you can get a sense of what factors may have affected the creative process. This can be especially useful if working within historical, biographical, or psychological types of criticism.

Depending on which theory you are applying, you can often find evidence in the film's dialogue, plot, setting, or sound track. You should also explore parts of the movie that seem to disprove your thesis and create an argument against them. As you do this, you might want to address what other critics have written about the movie. Their quotes may help support your claim.

Before you start analyzing a work, think about the different arguments made in this book. Reflect on how evidence supporting the thesis was presented. Did you find that some of the techniques used to back up the arguments were more convincing than others? Try these methods as you prove your thesis in your own critique.

When you are finished writing your critique, read it over carefully. Is your thesis statement understandable? Do the supporting arguments flow logically, with the topic of each paragraph clearly stated? Can you add any information that would present your readers with a stronger argument in favor of your thesis? Were you able to use quotes from the movie to enhance your ideas?

Did you see the work in a new light?

Timeline

1936 — Newman enrolls in Curtain Pullers at the Cleveland Play House.

1925 — Paul Newman is born on January 26 in Shaker Heights, Ohio.

1932 — Newman begins his acting career as court jester in a school play.

1943 — Newman graduates from Shaker Heights High School, attends Ohio University, and joins the U.S. Navy.

1969 — Newman plays Butch Cassidy in *Butch Cassidy and the Sundance Kid.*

1972 — Newman becomes a professional race car driver and eventually owns a racing team and a NASCAR Winston Cup car.

1982 — Newman establishes Newman's Own, a food line, and donates all its proceeds to charity.

1988 — Newman cofounds the Hole in the Wall Gang Camp in Ashford, Connecticut, for seriously ill children.

1986 — Newman stars in an Oscar-winning role as Fast Eddie Felson in *The Color of Money.*

1949
Newman graduates from Kenyon College in Ohio and marries Jackie Witte.

1954
Newman graduates from Yale University with a degree in drama. He studies drama at the Actors' Studio in New York City and begins his professional acting career on Broadway in *Picnic*.

Newman goes to Hollywood and stars in his first movie, *The Silver Chalice*.

1956
Newman plays boxer Rocky Graziano in *Somebody Up There Likes Me*.

1958
Newman stars with Elizabeth Taylor in *Cat on a Hot Tin Roof*.

After his first marriage ended in divorce, Newman marries actress Joanne Woodward.

1961
Newman stars in *The Hustler*.

1963
Hud is released, with Paul Newman in the title role.

1967
Newman stars as Lucas "Luke" Jackson in *Cool Hand Luke*.

1995
At age 70, Newman becomes the oldest driver to be part of a winning race team.

2006
Newman voices the character of Doc Hudson, the retired race car, in Disney's animated film *Cars*.

2008
Paul Newman dies on September 26, leaving a wife, five daughters, and two grandchildren.

HOLLYWOOD
PRODUCTION_____
DIRECTOR_____
CAMERA_____
DATE   SCENE   TAKE

Glossary

antihero
> A protagonist who is the opposite of a traditional hero type.

archetype
> A type of person or idea that has become so familiar that others can easily relate to it or copy it.

cynical
> Distrustful, sarcastic, negative, or skeptical of other people.

dysfunctional
> Not functioning normally.

ethical
> Conforming to accepted moral standards and principles of right and wrong.

hustle
> To obtain something by deceitful means; to swindle.

ironic
> Contrary to what is typically expected.

martyr
> One who chooses to suffer much for a belief or cause.

monologue
> A long speech made by one person.

nonconformist
> One who refuses to be bound by accepted customs, beliefs, or rules.

patriarch
The male head of a family or a tribe.

philanthropist
Someone who makes charitable donations in order to improve humanity.

psyche
The mind functioning as the center of thought, emotion, and behavior.

psychoanalysis
A method of studying the mind and mental or emotional disorders.

sham
Something fake or false.

stereotype
A traditional concept or type.

surrogate
One who takes the place of another; substitute.

tagline
A memorable phrase that sums up a film or a product.

vicariously
Indirectly through a substitute.

Bibliography of Works and Criticism

Important Works

The Silver Chalice, 1954

Somebody Up There Likes Me, 1956

The Rack, 1956

The Helen Morgan Story, 1957

Until They Sail, 1957

The Long, Hot Summer, 1958

The Left Handed Gun, 1958

Cat on a Hot Tin Roof, 1958

Rally 'Round the Flag, Boys!, 1958

The Young Philadelphians, 1959

From the Terrace, 1960

Exodus, 1960

The Hustler, 1961

Paris Blues, 1961

Sweet Bird of Youth, 1962

Hemingway's Adventures of a Young Man, 1962

Hud, 1963

A New Kind of Love, 1963

The Prize, 1963

What a Way to Go!, 1964

The Outrage, 1964

Lady L, 1965

Harper, 1966

Torn Curtain, 1966

Hombre, 1967

Cool Hand Luke, 1967

The Secret War of Harry Frigg, 1968

Winning, 1969

Butch Cassidy and the Sundance Kid, 1969

WUSA, 1970

Sometimes a Great Notion, 1971

Pocket Money, 1972

The Life and Times of Judge Roy Bean, 1972

The MacKintosh Man, 1973

The Sting, 1973

The Towering Inferno, 1974

The Drowning Pool, 1975

Buffalo Bill and the Indians, or Sitting Bull's History Lesson, 1976

Slap Shot, 1977

Quintet, 1979

When Time Ran Out, 1980

Fort Apache, the Bronx, 1981

Absence of Malice, 1981

The Verdict, 1982

Harry & Son, 1984

The Color of Money, 1986

Fat Man and Little Boy, 1989

Blaze, 1989

Mr. & Mrs. Bridge, 1990

The Hudsucker Proxy, 1994

Nobody's Fool, 1994

Twilight, 1998

Message in a Bottle, 1999

Where the Money Is, 2000

Road to Perdition, 2002

Magnificent Desolation:
   Walking on the Moon 3D,
   2005 (voice)

Cars, 2006 (voice)

Mater and the Ghostlight, 2006
   (voice)

Dale, 2007 (narrator)

Critical Discussions

Braudy, Leo, and Marshall Cohen, eds. *Film Theory and Criticism: Introductory Readings*. New York: Oxford University Press, 2009.

Godfrey, Lionel. *Paul Newman Superstar: A Critical Biography*. New York: St. Martin's Press, 1978.

Monaco, James. *How to Read a Film: Movies, Media, and Beyond: Art, Technology, Language, History, Theory*. New York: Oxford University Press, 2009.

Resources

Selected Bibliography

Butch Cassidy and the Sundance Kid. Dir. George Roy Hill. Twentieth Century Fox, 1969. DVD.

The Color of Money. Dir. Martin Scorsese. Touchstone Pictures, 1986. DVD.

Cool Hand Luke. Dir. Stuart Rosenberg. Warner Brothers Entertainment, 1967. DVD.

Hud. Dir. Martin Ritt. Paramount Pictures, Salem Productions, Inc., and Dover Productions, Inc., 1962. DVD.

Oumano, Elena. *Paul Newman*. New York: St. Martin's Press, 1989.

Further Readings

Levy, Shawn. *Paul Newman: A Life*. New York: Harmony Books, 2009.

Newman, Paul, and A. E. Hotchner. *Shameless Exploitation in Pursuit of the Common Good*. New York: Nan A. Talese, 2003.

Quirk, Lawrence J. *Paul Newman: A Life*. Lanham, MD: Taylor Trade Pub, 2009.

Web Links

To learn more about critiquing the roles of Paul Newman, visit ABDO Publishing Company online at **www.abdopublishing.com**. Web sites about the roles of Paul Newman are featured on our Book Links page. These links are routinely monitored and updated to provide the most current information available.

For More Information

The Academy of Motion Picture Arts and Sciences
8949 Wilshire Boulevard, Beverly Hills, CA 90211
310-247-3000
www.oscars.org

Read about the history of the Academy Awards and past winners.

Newman's Own Foundation
246 Post Road East, Suite 2C, Westport, CT 06880
www.newmansownfoundation.org

Find out more about Paul Newman and his commitment to donating money to those in need.

Source Notes

Chapter 1. Introduction to Critiques

None.

Chapter 2. A Closer Look at Paul Newman

None.

Chapter 3. An Overview of *Hud*

1. *Hud*. Dir. Martin Ritt. Paramount Pictures, Salem Productions, Inc. and Dover Productions, Inc., 1962.

2. Ibid.

3. Ibid.

4. Ibid.

5. Ibid.

Chapter 4. How to Apply Historical Criticism to *Hud*

1. Frank Manchel. *Film Study: An Analytical Bibliography, Volume 4*. London: Associate University Presses, 1990. 2260.

2. Bob Hinkle. "The Making of *Hud*." *American Legends Interviews*. 7 Dec. 2009 <http://www.americanlegends.com/ Interviews/bob_hinkle_making_of_hud.html>.

3. *Hud*. Dir. Martin Ritt. Paramount Pictures, Salem Productions, Inc. and Dover Productions, Inc., 1962.

4. Ibid.

5. Bosley Crowther. "HUD." *The New York Times*. 29 May 1963. 8 Feb. 2010 <http://movies.nytimes.com/movie/review?re s=EE05E7DF173CE26BBC4151DFB3668388679EDE>.

6. *Hud*. Dir. Martin Ritt. Paramount Pictures, Salem Productions, Inc. and Dover Productions, Inc., 1962.

7. Ibid.

Chapter 5. An Overview of *Cool Hand Luke*

1. *Cool Hand Luke*. Dir. Stuart Rosenberg. Warner Brothers Entertainment, 1967.

2. Ibid.

3. Ibid.

4. Ibid.

5. Ibid.

6. Ibid.

7. Ibid.

8. Ibid.

Chapter 6. How to Apply Archetypal Criticism to *Cool Hand Luke*

1. Tim Dirks. "Cool Hand Luke (1967)." *AMC Filmsite*. 5 Nov. 2009 <http://www.filmsite.org/cool.html>.

2. *Cool Hand Luke*. Dir. Stuart Rosenberg. Warner Brothers Entertainment, 1967.

3. Roger Ebert. "Cool Hand Luke." *rogerebert.com*. 3 Dec. 1967. 5 Nov. 2009 <http://rogerebert.suntimes.com/apps/pbcs. dll/article?AID=/19671203/REVIEWS/712030301/1023>.

4. Ibid.

5. Elena Oumano. *Paul Newman*. New York: St. Martin's Press, 1989. 109.

Source Notes Continued

Chapter 7. An Overview of *Butch Cassidy and the Sundance Kid*

1. Elena Oumano. *Paul Newman*. New York: St. Martin's Press, 1989. 123.

2. *Butch Cassidy and the Sundance Kid*. Dir. George Roy Hill. Twentieth Century Fox, 1969.

3. Ibid.

4. Ibid.

5. Ibid.

6. Ibid.

7. Ibid.

8. Ibid.

9. Ibid.

10. Ibid.

Chapter 8. How to Apply Gender Criticism to *Butch Cassidy and the Sundance Kid*

1. *Butch Cassidy and the Sundance Kid*. Dir. George Roy Hill. Twentieth Century Fox, 1969.

2. Ibid.

3. Ibid.

4. Ibid.

5. Ibid.

6. Ibid.

7. Ibid.

8. Ibid.

9. James Berardinelli. "Butch Cassidy and the Sundance Kid." *Reelviews Online*. 2001. 23 Feb. 2010 < http://www. reelviews.net/movies/b/butch_cassidy.html>.

10. Eve Kosofsky Sedgwick. *Between Men: English Literature and Male Homosocial Desire*. New York: Columbia University Press, 1985. 1.

Chapter 9. An Overview of *The Color of Money*

1. *The Color of Money*. Dir. Martin Scorsese. Touchstone Pictures, 1986.

2. Ibid.

3. Ibid.

4. Ibid.

5. Ibid.

Chapter 10. How to Apply Psychoanalytic Criticism to *The Color of Money*

1. *The Color of Money*. Dir. Martin Scorsese. Touchstone Pictures, 1986.

2. Ibid.

3. Richard Schickel. "Cinema: Kiss Shots off the Eight Ball." *Time Online*. 21 June 2005. 20 Apr. 2010 < http://www. time.com/time/magazine/article/0,9171,1075234,00.html>.

Index

About the Author

Sue Vander Hook has been writing and editing books for nearly 20 years. Her writing career began with several nonfiction books for adults and then focused on educational books for children and young adults. She especially enjoys writing about historical events and biographies of people who made a difference. Her published works also include a high school curriculum and series on disease, technology, and sports. Sue lives with her family in Mankato, Minnesota.

Photo Credits

Mark Kauffman/Getty Images, cover, 1; iStockphoto, cover; Marcela Barsse/iStockphoto, cover; AP Images, 12, 98 (top); Photofest, 17; Jim Ruymen, Reuters/Corbis, 21; Paramount Pictures/Photofest, 22, 27, 28, 35; Bettmann/Corbis, 40; Warner Bros./Photofest, 45, 48; Seven Arts, Warner Bros./ Photofest, 53; 20th Century Fox/Photofest, 60, 65, 66, 73, 98 (bottom); Buena Vista Pictures/Photofest, 78, 83, 84, 89; Michael Ochs Archives/Getty Images, 90